Sam & Mikey's Paper Airplanes

Marc Stevenson

Sam & Mikey's Paper Airplanes © 2023 by Marc Stevenson. All rights reserved. No part of this book may be used or reproduced in any manner whatsoever without written permission except in the case of reprints of reviews. For written permission write to:

                    Marc Stevenson

                    Email:
                    marcsvoice@gmail.com

Author: Marc Stevenson

Illustrator: Elly Mossman

Publisher: Tough Old Broad Publishing

Copyright © 2023 by Marc Stevenson

ISBN: 978-1990414-51-0

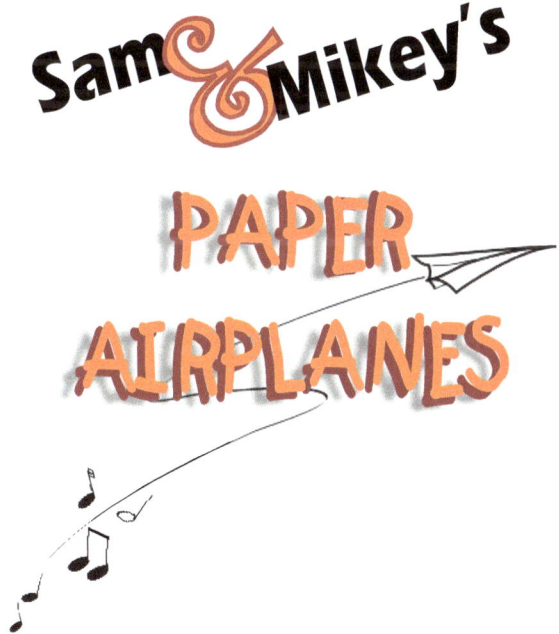

Sam & Mikey's Paper Airplanes

By Marc Stevenson

Publisher: Tough Old Broad Publishing

Sam & Mikey's Paper Airplanes

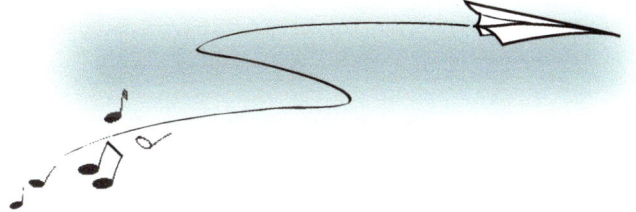

Samson loved Sundays. That's the day mom would go shopping and Sam and his little brother, Mikey went to Gram and Gramp's house for the afternoon.

They called it the Soundhouse because of all the noise they made over there. Downstairs there were lots of guitars to strum and drums to bang.

Sam liked playing Gramp's electric guitar. It had a bunch of pedals with lots of knobs and buttons that changed the sound. He turned every knob and pushed every button, until he knew exactly what they did.

One time he was playing so hard that his guitar pick went flying out of his hand, way across the room, and Gram snatched it right out of the air with her bare hands!

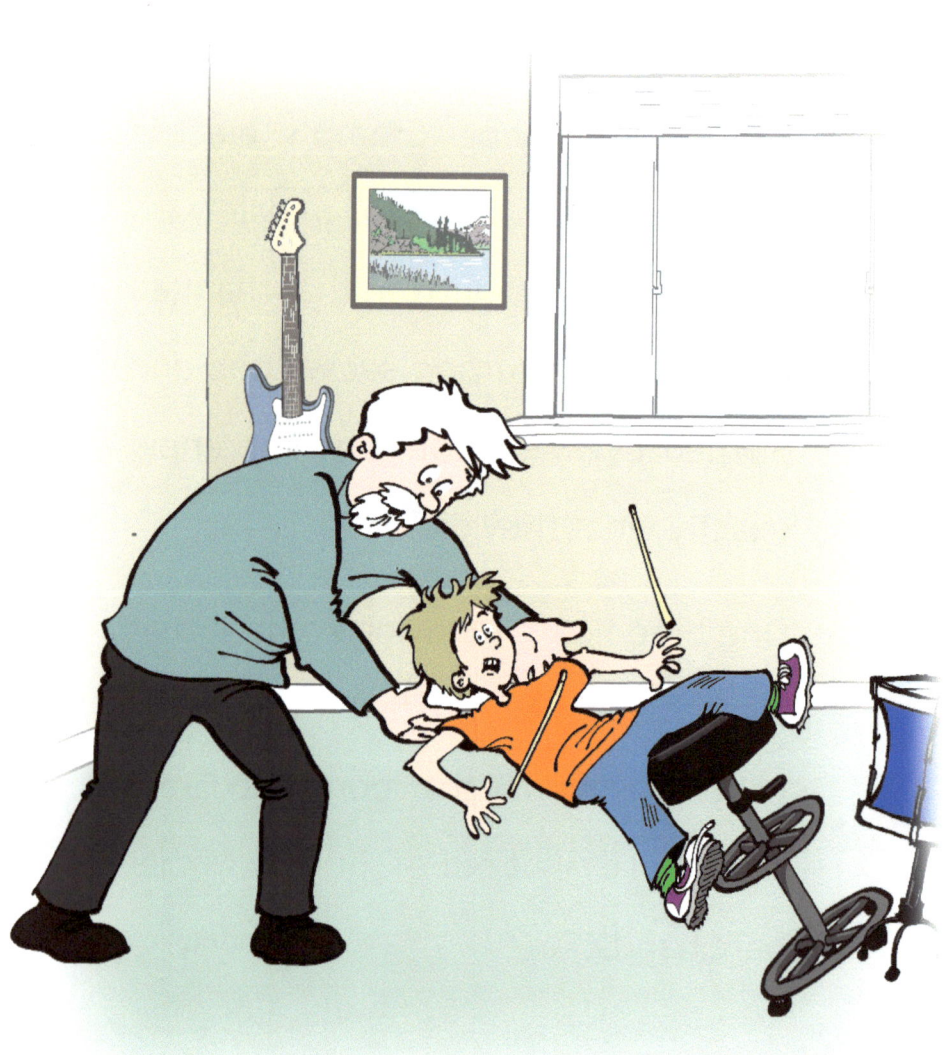

Mikey liked the drum kit with the big bass drum that he could kick with a pedal, and crashed all the cymbals with sticks. He loved to put on a show.

In the beginning he sat on Gramp's knee because he kept falling off the stool! He flung those sticks around so much that he hit Gramps right in the nose! Gramps taught him how to balance on the stool after that.

They played and played for lots and lots of Sundays, and what started as two brothers playing some things, turned into two brothers playing things together.

Then one Sunday, Sam and Mikey brought over a couple of friends.

Billy had a keyboard and Joe brought a microphone.

Then, they were a band, and they practised like crazy, writing lots of new songs, every Sunday for lots and lots of Sundays.

And they got really good!

They called their band *Paper Airplanes,* and before you knew it, they were playing concerts in stadiums all over the world.

Sam thought it would be a good time to learn how to fly a plane so he could get his band to every city they played.

There were lots of knobs and buttons and dials to play with in the cockpit too.

Sam's favourite place to fly was Australia because it's so far away and it has some really cool animals.

One time, they were playing an outdoor show near the big red rock, and a kangaroo jumped right up on stage! It jumped around so much that it knocked over the whole drum set.

It was just trying to find a way off the stage.

When they started playing at the Soundhouse they were just having fun, and they turned all that fun into a way to see the world and make music!

And when they were home ...

.. they still went to Gram and Gramps house every Sunday!